If He Was Mine

Also in the Series

The Mirror Told Me

The Mirror Told Me is the second volume of the *When Insecurities Speak Self-Development Series.* In *The Mirror Told Me,* the author walks individuals, both male and female, through a self-paced, self-development process. The words on the pages are written to encourage individuals to face their insecurities in a number of ways, including looking in the mirror. After all, isn't the first step to recovery admitting the truth? The truth is many people hide or cover up their insecurities rather than dealing with them face to face in order to rid themselves of the pain once and for all. The author uses practical and psychological methods and proven reasoning to rid deeply rooted, perpetually neglected insecurities that inhibit one's self-development, success, and ultimately lifelong happiness. Pick up a copy today and kiss that insecure man (or woman) in the mirror goodbye. Hasta la vista!

A Self-Development Series

When Insecurities Speak

Volume 1

If He Was Mine

Chakita Hargrove

with epigraph by Jino Ray

Heart Ink Press

Since 2008

Tallahassee • Plant City

© 2011 by Chakita Hargrove

All rights reserved. This book is protected under the copyright laws of the United States of America. This book may not be copied or reprinted for commercial gain or profit. No portion of this book may be reproduced, stored in a retrieval system, or transmitted in any form or by any means—electronic, mechanical, photocopy, recording, scanning, or other—without the prior written permission of the author. Brief quotations in critical reviews or articles are not permitted without the consent of the author. Permissions will be granted upon request. The use of short quotations and occasional copying for personal or group study is acceptable and encouraged.

Hargrove, Chakita. If he was mine/A self-development series/When insecurities speak/ Volume 1

ISBN: 978-0-9835854-2-8

HeartInkPress
www.heartinkpress.com
Tuned to the beat of your heart
Manifesting dreams and visions

Printed in the United States of America

Insecurity Defined

Insecurity is defined in several ways, which include

    1) Lacking self-confidence or assurance -- self doubting

    2) Being the quality or state of insecure, unstable, or shaky -- instability

    3) Being anxious or afraid -- not confident

    5) Being inadequately protected

    6) Feeling apprehension and uncertainty -- lacking assurance or stability

Purpose

The purpose of the *When Insecurities Speak* series is to address some issues that women face. This series will cover relationship issues, self-perception issues, and blaming issues. Most of the issues discussed in this series are deeply rooted in the lives of women, and women either deal with them internally or in the secret comforts of their rooms. Some women resort to journals and mirror conversations whereas some are able to talk openly with a limited number of people.

Insecurity is not an attribute that is only limited to women. There are many men who are also insecure, especially if they have experienced betrayal or if they perceive themselves to be the lesser individual in a relationship. However, most often it appears that women are the more insecure of the species.

Insecurity is damaging to a relationship especially when it is entirely unjustified. For example, women tend to take baggage from an old relationship into a new one and behave as if the new relationship is just like the previous un-dealt with relationships.

While most of us are insecure about something, be it our popularity, intelligence, or looks, we tend to deal with it and get on with our lives. We are aware that we are lacking in a certain department, but also reassure ourselves that we compensate for it in another area. Insecurity, no doubt, becomes a problem when it is unmanaged and verges on paranoia.

Because insecurities can wreak much havoc, I believe it is worth examining the problem and getting to the root of what causes the insecurity, just as any paranoia can be traced to certain deep-rooted fears.

Most often, insecurity stems from a basic lack of confidence, a feeling of just not being good enough and not being able to measure up to expectations, more from the woman herself, than from any external source. Sometimes a woman becomes insecure due to severe criticism or when a relationship goes sour.

Introduction

When insecurities are not dealt with they can stifle personal development and any healthy start or progression of a relationship. Within *If He Was Mine* you will find "Dear Diary" excerpts of a woman who is trying to find the one man for her. She is going about it the wrong way because instead of trying to deal with her insecurities she wants a man who can fill all her voids.

Day after day, week after week, she encounters various men and quickly falls for the ones who stop to entertain her desperateness. She distributes her phone number to gentlemen whose names she barely knows – Michael, no ... Sean. Wait, wait, wait, I know who it is. It's Charles.

When a woman chooses not to deal with her insecurities, she will be willing to settle for anything, especially if her principal desire is attention from a man. She will settle for one night stands and for abuse. She will even settle for a man who cheats on her because at least he does attend to her needs, if only but for a moment.

After each "Dear Diary" excerpt there is a "Question and Answer" section. Before you proceed to the next diary excerpt, you must take a moment to answer the questions. The most vital part of *If He Was Mine* is answering these questions. Each question is intended for you to manage, and possibly get rid of, your insecurities.

Once you have completed the excerpts, questions and answers, it is then time for self development and growth. This may not be a book you want to pass around because each question should be answered honestly. *If He Was Mine* should be treated like your personal journal or diary, a place where you are able to be honest with yourself and write down your most inner thoughts.

I hope that this "tool" helps you develop a better self-perception, that you are able to manage (or get rid of) your insecurities, and that you gain a better understanding of what a relationship should be by recognizing what it should not be.

Chakita S. Hargrove

Epigraph

Now, before I delve into my thoughts, let me first say that although I am speaking in terms of a woman's insecurities, the same holds true for the insecure man. Insecurities tend to manifest as similar behaviors in both women and men. With that being said, here is my take.

My experience has shown that when a woman is insecure, she tends to project the internal images created by her insecurities onto the man. By doing so, an environment of distrust is developed. Because the seed of insecurity has yielded a perception, she will tend to view every action of that man in light of the perception she has of him. This perception, of course, is the product of her insecurities, not his actions. What does that mean? For instance, if a woman has been cheated on in every relationship she has been in--or at least in the one(s) she was most invested in--she will naturally develop a defense mechanism that always has her on the lookout for signs of cheating. So, when she starts a new relationship, from day one she will be like a hound dog trying to sniff out any signs of infidelity, even if there are none to be found.

At times, she may even exaggerate the man's actions so that they will coincide with the fictitious images her insecurities have created within her mind. A simple phone call from an unknown caller will quickly become "the other woman." If he takes 15 minutes longer than normal to get home or to pick her up from work, she claims he was "an hour late" and that he must have been "doing something he ain't got no business doing." If his eyes wander in the general vicinity of another woman (who she perceives to be "prettier" than she) they MUST have been "all up in each other's faces." If he smiles and says thank you to the cashier, he was flirting. If he holds the door for another woman, he just wanted to look at her butt...and the list goes on. Her insecurities will lead her to assume the worst in every situation, thus creating undo stress in the budding relationship. As a result, the relationship will more than likely break down before the two ever really have an opportunity to build a strong foundation.

Now, there are times when the insecurities are valid based on the actions of the man. In such cases, it is not the responsibility of the man to change; no one can control his choices except him. In such cases, it is the responsibility of the woman to empower herself! Examine the situation and determine whether or not she should remain in a relationship with a man who feeds her insecurities and validates them with evidence. In such cases, so-called insecurities are no longer considered insecurities, they are considered warning signs! GET OUT BEFORE YOU SINK WITH THE SHIP!

Jino P. Ray, B.S.

Charles

Dear Diary,

Today was another long day. Traffic was crazy as ever but I managed to get a good parking space at work. Tonight I have my first date with Charles. He's the new guy at work whose office is on the third floor in accounting.

I met Charles last week in the elevator and he seems like the one. I know that I have been saying that a lot lately, but he really does seem like the guy for me. Tall, dark chocolate, built, and he has a great smile.

He knows how to keep my attention in conversation and I just think we are compatible. He is picking me up tonight at 8:00 p.m. to take me to some new restaurant downtown.

It's about time for me to get ready.

Until next time.

Women with insecurities tend to focus on quick, obvious, outer details about the opposite sex rather than spending time in getting to know the inner details about someone before deciding that he is "the one." Quick decisions are oftentimes inaccurate, which can lead to misunderstanding, hurt feelings, and wasted time.

With the Dear Diary excerpt above the writer, after only one week, concludes that she has met the one. How often have you thought that you have met the one only to find out that he wasn't the one at all?

It is necessary when dating or spending social time with a guy of interest to get to know more about the suitor than what is obvious or what you can perceive from the outer appearance.

Insecurities cause women to fall in love quickly and blind their eyes to tell-tell signs of "he is definitely not the one."

Question and Answer

1. Do you find yourself falling in love quickly? Why or why not?

_____
_____
_____
_____
_____
_____
_____
_____
_____
_____
_____
_____
_____
_____

2. What insecurities do you have about yourself?

_____
_____
_____
_____
_____
_____
_____
_____
_____
_____
_____
_____

Michael

Dear Diary,

I met this guy named Michael the other day at the mall. He was doing some shopping with three of his friends. He said they were planning a guys' weekend trip to Miami.

I gave him my number and told him to give me a call when he gets back in town.

Yes, I am getting to know Charles but we aren't officially dating. Michael seems like a good guy who enjoys life.

For him to go away for the weekend with the guys to have fun shows me that he knows how to let loose and not be consumed all the time with day-to-day stuff.

Until next time.

Women with insecurities are attracted to individuals who are capable of doing the things they wish they could do (e.g. stop allowing problems to have the power to consume them, go away on a vacation and have stress-free fun, et cetera).

The writer is so enthralled with the presumed spontaneity of Michael that she didn't ask probing questions: "Oh, what do you all plan to do in Miami?"

Before giving out your number, you should know the motives behind the exchange.

Women with insecurities tend to accept one-night stands. The main desire is to feel wanted and to be attended to.

Question and Answer

1. Have you ever entertained a guy just so you could have company or feel attended to? Why or why not?

_____
_____
_____
_____
_____
_____
_____
_____
_____
_____
_____
_____
_____
_____
_____
_____
_____
_____
_____
_____
_____
_____
_____
_____
_____
_____
_____
_____
_____
_____

2. How many sexual encounters have you had that led to nothing? How does that make you feel?

Charles

Dear Diary,

It has been about three weeks and Charles and I are still hanging out. I am noticing some small quirks about him but they aren't too major.

For instance, when we are at dinner he texts under the table and he never answers his phone. As a matter of fact, the nights he has stayed over the only sound I hear coming from his phone is the alarm.

I have asked why he ignores his calls when he is with me, and he simply says he wants to give me all of his attention. Now how sweet is that?!

Until next time.

Women with insecurities accept simplistic "pick-up lines," which distracts them from the obvious. If an individual you are getting to know never accepts a call in your presence, he is clearly hiding something.

The thing that is in hiding does not necessarily have to be another woman; it could be a child, an illegal job, or an undercover brotha'.

When people are insecure they fear being lonely, especially women who believe that a man is what they need. That a man, any man, can fill a void in their lives.

Question and Answer

1. Has a man ever told you something nice to distract you from noticing something or to stop you from asking questions? How long did it take you to figure that out? What did you do about it?

2. Have you ever used a man to fill a void? Why or why not?

Michael

Dear Diary,

It took Michael awhile, but he finally gave me a call. I thought that he blew me off. I started to think that I wasn't his type and that he and his boys were having a field day talking bad about me. I know I'm not the cutest thing in the world, but I'm not the ugliest either. I'm just glad he called.

He wanted to hook up later today but I told him today was a bad day because I had to work late.

The truth is today is Thursday, and on Thursdays Charles stays over.

Until next time.

Women with insecurities have distorted views of relationships. The writer wants to find the right man for herself but she is giving freely of herself every Thursday to Charles while still wanting to get to know Michael.

The woman has realized that Charles does not fill her void, but she keeps him because she has a routine with him. Her Thursdays are safe, and if no other man notices her, she knows that Thursday is soon to come.

So instead of ending the "getting to know" phase with Charles, she keeps him while expecting to get to know Michael.

Charles obviously does not fill her need of self-assurance if she thought that Michael's delayed call meant that he rejected her.

Women with insecurities don't like delays from men of interest.

Question and Answer

1. Have you ever gotten to know multiple guys at one time? Why or why not?

2. How does being rejected by a man make you feel?

Sean

Dear Diary,

I got bored today and decided to join a few online chat rooms. As soon as I posted my picture I started to get a lot of private chat requests.

I stayed online for about two hours, but I only gave one guy my number, Sean. Sean described himself as being outgoing, committed, and loyal. From his picture I could see that he was light-skinned and of average build.

Sean actually lives 15 minutes away, so we decided to meet up tomorrow night.

Until next time.

Many women with insecurities resort to online social networks because those venues allow them to embellish on the truth while trying to play it safe.

Most people choose to use their most flattering picture as their profile photo, even if the photo is outdated.

Lies usually immediately start at the beginning of a chat conversation because the insecure woman begins to answer questions the way she believes will get approval from the man.

What lies have you told in order to obtain approval?

This woman is seeking a relationship, she is obviously trying to fill her empty places, but she is not seeing that a man is not the answer. This woman has now added Sean to her web of insecurities.

Question and Answer

1. Have you ever used a social network to meet or chat with guys? Why or why not?

_____
_____
_____
_____
_____
_____
_____
_____
_____
_____
_____
_____
_____
_____
_____
_____
_____
_____
_____
_____
_____
_____
_____
_____
_____
_____
_____
_____
_____
_____

2. Have you ever gone on a blind date -- a date with a guy you really didn't know? If so, how did you feel leading up to the encounter? How did you feel when you met him face-to-face?

Michael

Dear Diary,

The strangest thing happened tonight. Michael and I were out walking down the "Strip" after dinner, and Sean called.

Of course I answered the call; shoot it was Sean. I'm not quite sure what all I said or how I sounded, but when I hung up the phone, Michael grabbed my arm extremely tight and told me that I better not be talking to any other dude.

Of course I lied and told him that I wasn't. Dang, I got this dude jealous! My arm is still a little sore.

Until next time.

Because the woman desperately wants the attention of a man, she doesn't address Michael about how he grabbed her.

She simply goes with the flow and makes herself believe that she has him jealous.

Women with insecurities mentally minimize confrontations, threats, and physical abuse just so the man won't leave.

In her mind, if he leaves she has nothing, no one loves her, and she is not attractive.

"Small" confrontational moments can develop into bigger ones if they are not addressed from the beginning and if they are not addressed correctly.

Once abuse is overlooked, the man will believe that it is acceptable, and he realizes that the woman is weak.

Question and Answer

1. Have you ever been in a relationship that had any level of abuse? If so, what happened? How did you get out?

2. What is your definition of abuse? Is there any abuse you are willing to take?

Sean

Dear Diary,

I finally met up with Sean, and let me just say that he is definitely the one.

Now I know I said that Charles was the one, and that he was just how I like them -- tall and dark chocolate. But Sean is awesome.

He may be light-skinned and average-sized; however, I feel a connection with him.

He didn't joke about going back to my place or his place. When he talks I am mesmerized.

But before I get rid of Michael and Charles, I have to see where this is going.

Until next time.

This woman of insecurities really wants all three men in one. With Sean, she doesn't have to worry about having sex or avoiding physical roughness.

If she really thought Sean was the one, she shouldn't be hesitant to get rid of the other two.

Women with insecurities are complex and often times make no sense when rationalizing decisions.

Sean is opposite the physical attraction she has with Charles, and he is less aggressive-- masculine-- than Michael. But what makes Sean the one is that he is not like the other two. Insecurities are causing this woman to be complex.

Question and Answer

1. Have you ever been afraid to let go of a man? Why or why not?

2. Have your insecurities ever gotten in the way of a relationship? How so?

Self-Development and Growth

Before you complete this section, take a moment to review your previous answers. If you skipped any questions, please go back and answer them wholly. The purpose of this section is to build from your self-evaluation. If you have completed all prior questions, let's move on.

The insecurities dealt with in the Dear Diary excerpts were insecurities that affected the writer's ability to establish a healthy relationship with a man. Hopefully, throughout the Question and Answer sections you have developed some type of awareness of your own insecurities that could be affecting your present relationship or any future relationship.

Many people jump into relationships without knowing what they really want. Relationships are jumbled when an individual is trying to figure out what he or she wants while being in the relationship. If the individual chooses to carry past relationships, more problems can arise.

What I would like for you to do is review all of your insecurities that you have listed throughout *If He Was Mine*. If there are more insecurities that came to your mind, please write those down. Below, I want you to take some time and write down or map-out how you will manage or get rid of these insecurities.

_____
_____
_____
_____
_____
_____
_____
_____
_____
_____
_____
_____
_____
_____
_____
_____
_____
_____
_____
_____
_____
_____
_____

Now that you have devised a plan of action to manage or rid your insecurities, you have to commit yourself to making sure that you overcome your insecurities.

In the "Purpose" of *If He Was Mine*, I stated that insecurity can stem from a basic lack of confidence, a feeling of just not being good enough and not being able to measure up to expectations. These types of insecurities usually come more from the woman herself than from any external source. At this moment, I want you to think of (and write below) the type of circumstances or environments that cause you to be insecure. For instance, sometimes a woman becomes insecure due to severe criticism or when a relationship goes sour. I, then, want you to mention below how you will not allow these (or other) circumstances and environments to have that much power over you. For example, you will no longer let the company of couples make you feel unwanted.

The last thing I want you to consider is the type of relationship you want to have. Do you really know what type of relationship you want? Some women are satisfied with relationships with no commitment. Some women set standards for a relationship that they are unwilling to prepare themselves for. When a woman thinks of what a man should offer in a relationship, she must understand that the man may be expecting the woman to offer certain things as well.

I want you to take some time to write down the type of relationship you want, and then I want you to write down what you can offer in the relationship.

I hope that *If He Was Mine* was a useful tool for you. Please send comments to the author at chakita@freshwindenterprises.com.

If you would like to have the author as a guest speaker, or host an *If He Was Mine* session, or if you would like to have a counseling session, please send all requests to info@freshwindenterprises.com.

More copies of *If He Was Mine* can be purchased in the library at:
www.heartinkpress.com

Certificate of Completion

is presented to

_____

for

Completing the If He Was Mine volume of When
Insecurities Speak, a Self-Development Series.

Chakita Hargrave, CEO
_____   _____
Signature   Date

Fresh Wind Enterprises LLC

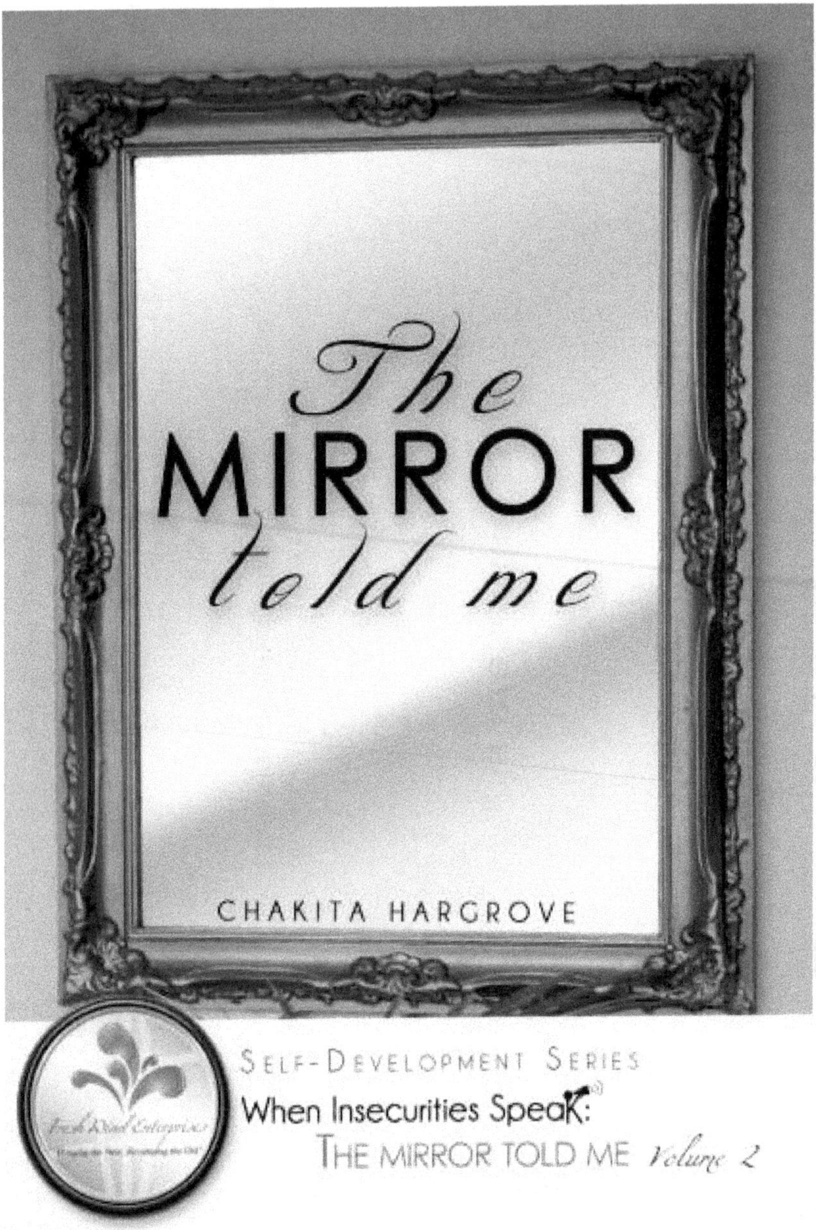

The MIRROR told me

CHAKITA HARGROVE

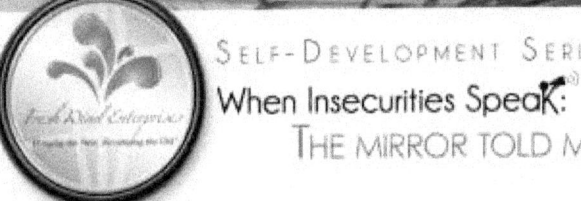

SELF-DEVELOPMENT SERIES
When Insecurities Speak:
THE MIRROR TOLD ME *Volume 2*

www.ingramcontent.com/pod-product-compliance
Lightning Source LLC
Chambersburg PA
CBHW061259040426
42444CB00010B/2419